The Bear Safety Primer

A Guide on How to Live in Harmony and Safety with Bears

By

CJ Hernley

(Author of: A Handful of Idiots
and a Bunch of Bears)

ISBN-13:
978-1482008180

ISBN-10:
1482008181

Table of Contents

Dedication

To those who believe it is possible to live in harmony with bears and are willing to devote themselves to doing what it takes to ensure the safety and well-being of both people and bears.

Introduction

In the USA, we have three species of bears. The Polar Bear, the Grizzly or Brown Bear, and Black Bears. Polar bears are always blondes, Grizzlies and Black Bears come in every shade from blonde to brown and black, and all the various red and orange tones in between. I have no idea why these bears were given common names that may or may not have anything to do with their fur color, but I guess we'll just have to live with that. I am going to drop the capitalization of these common names, mainly because I'm just lazy. I will be referring to most bears as "him" for the sake of convenience. This is not to imply that "he" bears are any more or less rascally than "she" bears. It's a toss-up.

In Alaska we refer to most inland brown bears as "grizzlies". They are a smaller race of bears than their bigger coastal cousins. If a grizzly resides on the coast, we call it a brown bear or a "brownie." So bear terminology in Alaska can be very regional. Black bears are everywhere but the far frozen north, and they are going to be the bear of concern for those who reside in the lower 48 states as well of much of Alaska. Grizzly bears are in very short supply everywhere but Alaska. Polar bears are more of a marine mammal and an ice pack dweller than a terrestrial. I do not consider myself to be an authority on this species. Since most types of bears have a lot more in common with one another than differences, I am going to simply talk about "bears" in general for the most part.

Much of the safety information you will find in this book was derived from my other book, "A Handful of Idiots and a Bunch of Bears." I have attempted to compress it down to the essential essence of the matter. I have added more information for those who actually live in bear country and disclosed the vegetable that constitutes the bear's version of catnip. In addition, I have tried to restrain myself from telling funny bear tales to keep this booklet compact, but I haven't been entirely successful. Sorry! If you like that sort of thing, please see my other book. It's full of it...

Preface

I have lived in the central coastal Alaskan bush for 28years and have spent much of my time "playing with bears" and test driving all manner of theory on bear behavior and deterrents. I am an avid backpacker, beachcomber and camping enthusiast with access to a private airplane. This has gotten me out into remote reaches of wilderness that few have seen. There, I often camp and wander in solitude. Sometimes, if I am lucky, family or friends will join me on these wild and crazy adventures.

I have survived four bear charges and two predatory encounters, all well described in my other book, "A Handful of Idiots and a Bunch of Bears." Since my need to test and understand bear behavior has gotten me into trouble on quite a few occasions, I won't be offended if you think I'm an idiot, or at least a little insane. I am ok with that. But what should interest you even more is that I don't have a scratch on me. That might be because I have exceedingly good luck. Or perhaps it could be I have come up with some very workable solutions to interacting with bears safely. Ultimately, I'll leave it up to you, the reader, to decide.

Chapter 1   BEAR BASICS:

WHAT YOU NEED TO KNOW

Myths and Misinformation

It is shocking that much of the information published about bears is simply incorrect or misleading. Bears are the victims of the movie industry and the internet. Both abound with misguided nonsense. Let's examine the facts and fiction and see if we can come to some reasonable conclusions.

1. Who said bears can't climb trees? All species of bears can climb trees. It is not a safe place for you to go if you meet a bear. It will be interpreted as a submissive gesture and this can have serious consequences for you. If you go up a tree you must be prepared to defend yourself when they come up after you.

2. Who said bears can't run downhill? A moron, no doubt. Bears can hit speeds of over 30 mph in a short sprint. A bear can run up a hill, down a hill, or sideways on a hill. You can't outrun a bear unless you have a huge head start and somewhere safe nearby to run to. Running from a bear triggers the predator/prey response in a bear. Trust me, you don't want to do that!

3. What fool said never look a bear in the eye? To avert your eyes is both an act of stupidity and a dangerous submissive gesture. It is imperative you don't appear submissive to a bear. This avert your eyes nonsense came about as an idea to help appease an agitated mother bear. I wholeheartedly disagree. I always look right at a mama bear, or any other bear. So, if you find a bear looking at you, look right back. There is simply no other way to understand what is happening and what may befall you next. Always show appropriate dominance.

4. It's winter, no worries, the bears are hibernating. Not true, not true, not true. Well, most of them are "sleeping it off" in colder climates, but not all of them. There are bears

who come out of hibernation to stretch their legs and walk around a bit. There are bears who never seem to hibernate at all. There are bears who just do some heavy napping in strange places before they commit themselves to a proper den. Just because it's the dead of winter, you cannot be positively, 100% sure, you are in a bear-free zone. You have no way of knowing, if, when, or where, a bear will decide to bed down for the winter. We just hope they do.

5. Mother bears are always dangerous. Not always, and especially not black bears. Black bear mothers are sometimes both submissive and defensive, but only rarely aggressive. They don't usually attack, even when you get between them and their cubs. Brown bear mamas can be a little more of a handful. But her behavior will usually be defensive in nature and that is a good thing. It is true that it's not a good idea to get between a brown bear mother and her cubs, but it isn't always fatal by any means.

6. A bear charging you is a bear attacking you. Wrong again! This is why so many bears get shot. Everyone thinks a bear charging you is an act of potentially fatal aggression, but this

is not usually the case. I have been charged by big Kodiak brownies on four separate occasions. Not one of them intended to kill me or I wouldn't be writing this book. During a bear charge, a person may behave inappropriately and manage to get themselves mauled or killed, but appropriate defense training can prevent that. So let's get educated!

7. If a bear attacks you, play dead. Very bad advice! Never play dead unless you want to end up that way for real. If you find yourself being mauled by a bear and you are unable to fight, going into the "bear defensive posture" is a better bet for survival. We'll be discussing that.

8. There is safety in numbers. Maybe. It is logical to assume if there are lots of people around, a bear will be more likely to steer clear of you. I think this is often the case, but not always. Bears can, and will charge large numbers of people, especially if they are guarding a cache. Of course, being charged isn't the end of the world if you behave yourself. Regardless, always be vigilant in bear country, no matter how many of you there are in your group.

9. A bear up on his hind legs is acting aggressively. Wrong, again. You may have been watching too many movies that depict bears standing up just before they attack. This isn't quite correct in real life. A bear stands up on hind legs to see better and scan the breeze for scent clues. In this situation, he is just checking out the scene. This is an act of curiosity, not aggression.

10. Who started the rumor that bears have poor eye sight? It's not true, their sight is roughly equivalent to people. They also have especially good night vision. Bears can also see in color and most animals can't. They have better noses than bloodhounds and they have very acute hearing too. I think this rumor got started because bears can easily get distracted and don't always pay attention to every detail of their environment when they are focused on something else. Sometimes they seem lost in their thoughts.

11. Bear bells will scare bears away. I wish I could tell you that this is true, but it isn't. Bears are very curious and intelligent animals. This is why using sound deterrents can sometimes backfire on you. In some

situations, tinkling bells or singing might actually bring them to you for a look-see.

Warning sounds should always be used when you are in low visibility situations to prevent unwanted surprises. I have had my best luck with a friendly shout. Keep your voice deep and low. Or you can clap your hands every fifty feet, whatever you prefer.

12. Guns or pepper spray, you need to have them! Yes, but why use either one of these as your primary bear defense? They require skill, expertise and training to utilize them safely and correctly. I have had both the training and practice, so they are an important part of my back up system, but I have never had to resort to actually using either one.

My primary defenses involves a dominant retreat I like to call "bear dancing," and a lung driven safety horn. Don't get me wrong. Training and practice is required to use these safe and sane deterrents correctly too. However, please note an important feature. They will not kill or harm anyone accidently, and they are more effective deterrents by a long shot! This is a very bold statement and will no doubt inspire controversy. People who do not reach for guns or bear spray as their primary defense have been largely ignored or laughed off as eccentric idiots. This is unfortunate because some of us have actually figured out how to safely defend ourselves, armed or not. For me, my system has withstood the test of time in countless numbers of close encounters, four charges and two predatory events. Your best advice should be coming from those who keep walking away from close encounters without a scratch. It's a real bonus in my opinion, when the bear gets to walk away too.

13. Don't go into bear country while menstruating. Well, being a woman, I can state with confidence most bears have little interest in my bodily fluids. Since menstrual fluids contain blood, this looks like a paradox. Let's just say you shouldn't get sloppy about it. Use internal protection, discard or burn the remains well away from camp. But don't get paranoid. I never stayed home because I was menstruating. I have experienced predatory behavior, but not during menstruation.

Chapter 2   CLOSE ENCOUNTERS AND

CHARGES

Lets jump right into the meat of the matter. The thing that worries people most about bears is ending up too close for comfort with one. Since I can measure quite a few of my close encounters in mere inches, let me reassure you that most of these adventures with bears can, and will, have happy endings. The best defense in a tight situation is having a good understanding of how bears operate. I'm going to teach you how to evaluate a bear's mental state and how to dance with them if they want to rumba.

Let's start with some simple statistical facts. 95% of all bears you encounter are minding their own business and want nothing to do with you. You will hear a rustle in the brush as they get out of your way. If you are lucky, you might spot a backside vanishing into the distance. This is a typical bear sighting, no actual "encounter" is even involved. I love seeing bears and long ago gave up trying to tally the countless numbers of bears that have successfully removed themselves from the scene before I could get a good look. Seeing bears up close is truly a privilege that not many people get to experience. I have had the good fortune to live in areas like Afognak Island where bears were a part of my everyday life for years. Count yourself lucky if you get to observe bears. (Hopefully from a healthy distance.)

Then there are the other 5% of bears. They comprise true encounters of the more up close and personal kind. Most of these will be what we call "defensive encounters." You will have somehow managed to stumble into a bear that was snoozing and startled them awake. Or you might blunder into a bear that is guarding a food source or a meaty cache. Be it a salmon stream or berry patch, always be aware that bears can sometimes be touchy about competition and sharing of food resources. Then there are mama bears. Some are quite willing to defend their cubs if they feel threatened. The simple solution to avoid all defensive encounters is to be aware of bears and make them aware of you. Make some noise! Loud deep shouts and hand clapping should always be employed when you are in bear country, especially in brushy and low visibility situations. The one thing that all of these situations has in common is the element of surprise. Never surprise a bear and you will never have any problems. Well almost.

The other area of wrongful human liability is food. We have it, they want it. Whether it's the lunch in your knapsack, the fish you just caught, or simply a carrot in your garden, you are possibly inviting trouble with a bear. This is what can be categorized as a "foraging and procurement" encounter. Bears are opportunistic diners and they wander around for miles looking for something tasty. If they come across anything they consider as potentially edible, they see it as their mission to procure the resource. If it's in your tent, whose fault is that? It's yours! Don't mess around with any of a bear's potential food resources and don't provide them either. They will eat anything we will and whole lot of disgusting stuff we won't. They love carrion, sewage and garbage too. By our standards, bears don't have any at all, so keep that in mind.

Almost everything I am going to talk about in this book will be because you have screwed up and managed to tempt, surprise, or stimulate a bear. Who goofed up? You did, pay attention!

The last and rarest of all encounters is the predatory one. These are much less than 1% of all the bears you could possibly meet. Most people who spend all their lives living and recreating in bear habitat will never see this. It is the rarest of the rare exception to meet a bear that wants to eat you. Most bears do not deem humans a potential menu item. Considering they will eat almost anything else on the face of the earth, this is pretty remarkable. We should count ourselves very lucky. There is always an exception to the rule however, so I am going to cover this improbable event too.

Inadvertently Triggering the Predator/Prey Response

This is another situation that education can really help prevent. Bears are scary to most people. Fear causes us to act like "prey." Acting like prey triggers the predator instinct in bears. This can cause you to get mauled, killed or eaten. The following are prey behaviors. You are going to want to avoid ever doing any of them while in the presence of a bear.

1. A high pitched yelp or screaming

2. Panting, heavy breathing or hyperventilating

3. Frantic motion, running or fleeing

4. Expelling urine, feces or vomit

5. Freezing in terrified panic, becoming unresponsive, or fainting.

It is simple. Don't act like a bear's dinner! Being terrified during a close encounter with a bear is very natural, but it is all about your acting skills. Teach yourself to keep your voice low, deep and loud. Take slow deep breaths as quietly as possible. This is no time to imitate Darth Vader! Retreat slowly while making deliberate dominant motions at the bear. This is what I like to call the "bear dance." It creates a natural cautionary hesitation in the bear and discourages him from making any actual physical contact with you. You create a safe exit strategy in a tight situation and you can waltz away from the hairiest of close encounters.

Do you ever wonder why news reports about a mauling usually start with a headline that includes a biker or a jogger? These unfortunate people have managed to inadvertently stimulate a predator/prey response in a bear that was probably minding his own business when they happened into his presence. Snap! The motion and the heavy breathing switch the bear into predator mode and he responds instantly. The bear is probably just as surprised as the person he is attacking! If the human victim escalates the situation with frantic screaming or going into playing dead mode, it will be difficult to keep the bear from doing a lot of damage in the excitement of the moment. Sometimes they come to their senses and back off, sometimes not. This is when fighting a bear becomes very important. An aggressive bear can back off when things start to happen that don't make sense to him. That moment of hesitation is the opportunity to begin a dominant retreat if you're able to. Dance on out of there!

Bears Meeting Bears

Let's start by talking about how bears deal with one another in nature. Bears are for the most part non-confrontational when they meet their own kind. If they meet a bear they are acquainted with they will often greet each other by touching noses and they might opt to spend some time together, especially if there are some family ties. But most bears who are unacquainted are content to size each other up briefly and then get on about their business.

In a tense situation when bears first approach one another, they will be trying to establish their opponents identity with scent clues. They might rise to their hind legs to evaluate their nemesis, approaching in small fits and starts. They will move toward one another cautiously, somewhat like angry dogs woofing and snarling. They will pause to show their side views to their opponents, the "do you want a piece of this?" pose. Having served notice on one another in this manner, a few bluff charges might happen. Usually at this point, one chooses to exit and is allowed to do so. All of these behaviors I have just described are forms of posturing and negotiating. This is how bears sort out their dominance issues. The alpha bear gets first choice in where to fish or what part of a carcass he wants to devour. Or if there isn't enough to share, he takes it all. Or if cupid is involved, the big, bad boy is likely to get lucky, wink!

There are only a few circumstances where things get tense between bears. Food and sex pretty much sum it up, no surprise there. Bears will establish a pecking order when a food resource is large enough to share, such as a salmon stream or a whale carcass. Sometimes this can get a little messy, but there usually aren't any fatalities in sorting out the chow line. Often, large boars (males) will be the instigators of trouble when settling food control issues. Testosterone and trouble, they often go hand in hand.

Bears Fighting

Sometimes the competition for food or sex escalates into a fight if no one is willing to yield. Once again, this is ugly, but only very rarely fatal. There will be cuffing and biting and sometimes bears will lock up like wrestlers while trying to get the advantage. It is an amazing demonstration of strength and courage. It is all over once one of them yields and exits the scene.

Mama bears defending their cubs from potentially predatory behavior of other bears is another instance where threats and posturing is used. (Yes, bears can become cannibals in difficult times.) This is also an example of size not being the main issue. A small mama bear with big attitude can sometimes force a much larger bear to yield.

The amazing part about bear squabbles is that most things are usually sorted out without actual physical contact. This important characteristic of bears is what I base the defensive exit strategy on.

Defensive Bears

So what does a defensive bear look like? He looks aggressive! He may swat the ground or a bush with his paw. His ears will be laid back like a dog. He may be woofing or growling. He will look at you in glances. He may show you his side view. His jaws may be agape, popping, or drooling. His approach can be a full on charge without warning, or a series of small bluff charges getting closer each time. The bear isn't attacking you, he is communicating with you. You are being put on notice, you are being warned.

How you are responding to him will dictate his next move. There will be no question in your mind that you are in big trouble, but you're not as bad off as it looks! This is a situation that can usually be resolved with the dominant exit strategy I like to call the "bear dance." If this doesn't do it, your horn, your bear spray, or your gun will. In that exact order please. More ahead.

The Predatory Approach

A bear in a predatory mode is a whole different animal. First, the approach is going to both bold and alert. The ears will be up and the eyes fixated on you. The bear will advance on you slowly as in the manner of stalking you. Or aggressively, as in a predator in the process of chasing you down. The bear will be silent, head forward and very intent. Some people who have witnessed this behavior have not lived to tell about it. Strangely, a bear in predatory mode doesn't appear at first glance to be doing anything that is obviously frightening other than coming closer to you. But this is a bear that wants to have you for dinner. If you see it coming, you have a good chance of surviving it, even unarmed. If you don't see it coming and you are ambushed, you can still live to tell about it if you fight for your life.

Defend Yourself!

How to Defend Yourself in any Situation ? If the space between you in the bear allow it, dance First! This may seem controversial, but it has been my most practiced defense. Dancing with Bears is the best initial defense against a bear that is misbehaving. A bear that is misbehaving is any bear that isn't running away from you like a proper bear should.

The bear dance should always begin with an introduction. As soon as you spot a bear, you should speak or shout out a greeting in a nice, low voice. Emphasis on *deep* and *loud*. "Hey bear!" Then, you might want to wave an arm slowly overhead and extended to help him sort you out from the background. Most bears will be well on their way by now.

Let's say he is hesitating at this point. Perhaps he is curious or confused by your presence. Clap your hands several times as loud as you can. If the bear hasn't left by now, a situation might be developing. I want you to stomp the ground as hard as you can and slap your thigh as loudly as possible several times. You have just gotten the bear's attention and you have put him on notice. Usually, your dance partner is long gone by now. Then you can pat yourself on the back for a job well done. This is how ninety five out of a hundred bear sightings go. A quick hello and they are gone.

Dance With Me!

But let's say the bear wants to get up close and personal instead. This is unusual, but it does happen in less than five percent of encounters. The closer a bear gets, the more careful you need to be. As soon as you shout out your initial greeting and have started your dancing retreat, if the bear has not immediately left, it is time to get "loaded for bear." Put your bear horn in your mouth and clench it firmly in your teeth ready to use. This leaves your hands free to get your bear spray out, aimed and ready. This is the trickiest part of the dance and it is good to practice this many times so you know the routine, even in a panic. (We have not covered these bear deterrents yet, but we will.) You are now slowly walking backwards in retreat with two different deterrents at the ready; stomp, slap, stomp, slap! This should appease the bear if he is defending something or is demonstrating dominance. Usually, the bear lets you exit, no questions asked. Yes, this works well on mama bears with cubs too.

Now You're in Trouble...

But let's say your bear still wants to tango. You have a very determined defensive situation and/or they are sizing you up for a meal. The defensive situation is not unusual, but being viewed as a potential dinner, is. We have now entered the realm of that rare 1 to 2 percent of bears that seem incorrigible. You are now dancing away with at least two different bear deterrents at ready. Keep your eyes on the bear and continue steadily backing up, *slowly*. If things go wrong, you need to be ready. If the bear initiates a charge, stand your ground or advance a few steps and be ready to deploy both the horn and the bear spray as soon as he enters your personal space, about 15 to 20 feet away.

Holding your ground or advancing shows dominance, and this will cause him to feel reluctant to make actual physical contact with you. Wait until the last possible moment to use your horn or spray. They are most effective when there is an element of surprise to them. The bear might kick dirt on you when he turns from a full on charge, but he will turn or veer off. Be ready, and keep facing him just in case he wants to bluff charge you a couple times. Usually they give up long before this point unless there is something very important at stake such as threatened cubs or an important food source.

Somebody has got to leave the scene of the confrontation. If he isn't budging, it needs to be you. Do not hang around near the scene of the crime once the face off seems to be over. Get out of there, preferably back in the direction you just came from. (This is to avoid whatever it is the bear might have been defending.)

Doing the bear dance has probably saved me too many times to count. It works well with aggressive and dominant bears and with defensive and irritated bears. It is certainly better than nothing if you should have the misfortune of running into a predatory bear. When you dance with a bear, your motions are letting the bear know you are unafraid, yet willing to yield. You are saying, "don't tread on me, I'm leaving." You waltz away, to dance again another day.

A Bad Surprise

Sometimes you can surprise a bear when he is napping. This of course wouldn't happen if you were properly using your deep, loud voice or using hand claps to signal your presence. In an open space the bear will most likely flee. In a tight brushy situation you might inspire a sudden defensive charge. Regardless of how you have ended up being so close to a bear, if he is already in your personal space, 10 to 25 feet away or less, you need to skip the dance, immediately use your horn, and be reaching for your spray. Don't just toot the horn, do a long blast. A horn used this close actually hurts the bears ears. They will at least back up shaking their heads while they sort out their next move. Now you begin your dancing retreat. You more than likely will not need your bear spray, but have it ready as you back away. Once again, notice, notify and be "bear aware." These types of encounters are totally avoidable!

Ambushes

Another rare option is for a bear to ambush you. There is an old saying among hikers and hunters; "The first one on the trail, and the last on the trail are the most vulnerable, so, be the guy in the middle." This saying is in reference to being ambushed by a bear, be glad it is a very rare occurrence.

Most ambushes are of the foraging and procurement type. You have something the bear wants. The fish on your stringer, the deer you are dragging home for dinner, the peanut butter sandwich in your hand. These ambushes have to be considered predatory in nature even though you might not be the main focus. Rarer yet, the bear that thinks you should be his dinner. Any bear in a predatory mood is a very dangerous bear. This kind of bear will be very persistent in its pursuit of a meal. He is likely to come back repeatedly, even if it seems you have run him off. Worse yet, if this bear decides to focus on you instead, you are in serious trouble.

Some people who feel they have been ambushed were probably the victims of a surprised bear. This is by far a more common situation than a true predatory ambush. Regardless, get that horn into your mouth and let them have it! If it is a true ambush rather than a surprised bear, you are very justified in using a gun in this situation. The trouble is telling the difference in a pinch. The surprised bear usually comes at you from the front. You are being charged. A true ambush is more likely going to come from behind you.

Strangely, many so called ambushes aren't personal. A bear wants that deer you are dragging out or the fish you just caught. Once you have been robbed, you are often free to go. Dance you're lucky little ass right on out of there! Please let the authorities know about this bear. The area needs to be posted and closed so others won't be inadvertently getting cheap thrills from this outlaw. Once a bear starts down this sorry path, it only gets worse. You probably weren't his first, and you almost assuredly won't be his last.

The Bear Dance as a Deterrent

Why does the bear dance work with such amazing consistency? Because the dance imitates the motions a bear makes during an unpleasant confrontation with another bear. When a bear is agitated he will sometimes swat the ground. You are doing the equivalent thing when you stomp your foot, or slap your thigh. It is a message of warning and you are giving it right back to him. Bears use these challenges and body language to size each other up. Opinions on dominance and submissiveness between bears are usually rendered without violence. That's the good news! We are betting on that trait to get us out of a close encounter of scariest kind in one piece. It often resolves confrontational situations without guns or violence. I have also used it successfully when I was without bear deterrents or weapons of any kind. I turned one Kodiak brownie charge away from me using the dance only. Variations of the bear dance suit almost any situation you can find yourself including the next one.

Predatory Bear Experiences

More people are killed by dogs than bears. Is anyone getting hysterical about this? Of course not. What about moose? They tend to get very testy in the wintertime and I have been charged twice while out cross country skiing. I consider them more dangerous than bears and they scare me even more. I'd rather be charged by a bear, at least I feel like I understand them. A 1,200 lb vegetarian wanting to kick me into oblivion is a whole other matter! What's up with that?

Having said this, I have personally experienced truly predatory incidents with bears only twice in 28 years of fooling around with them. So, it isn't impossible for it to occur, just extremely unlikely. Since I am here to tell you about it, it is safe to say a predatory event can be very survivable. Yes, the worst thing imaginable can have a happy ending, if you need the gory proof, please see my other book.

Playing Dead Can get you Killed

Playing dead sometimes gets you dead. The old fashioned notion of throwing yourself on the ground, face down, with your hands clasped behind your neck and then going limp, is not only almost impossible to do, it's insane! Clasping your hands behind your neck leaves all the rest of your body vulnerable to damage from being mauled and it can have truly hideous results. Hands aren't much protection to begin with, and your entire spinal column is exposed. Thinking that you can pull off feigning death while an animal rips you apart will possibly lead to you not having to fake it anymore. If you find yourself in this sorry situation, without any other options, please assume the "defensive position" instead. Never play dead!

The Defensive Position

The defensive position is a tight fetal pose lying on your side with knees tucked as high into your core as you can get them. Your hands should be clasped tightly around the back of your neck. Clench your arms tightly to the sides of your head, with elbows touching together in front of your face, if you can. Your chin is tucked tightly to your chest. You are trying to protect your face, scalp and neck with your arms and hands. You protect your spine by being on your side, and your internal organs with your legs up tight, to you. This is not playing dead so much as rolling yourself up tight like a hedgehog. A bear might paw you around or give you a bite to be sure you are not a threat. Your adrenaline levels will help make this more bearable, ooh - bad pun! If a grizzly mama has you down, this is a viable option. Otherwise you should be fighting!

Charge On!

There's nothing quite like being charged by a bear! Your heart pounds, your mouth goes dry and time seems to flow in slow motion. It's all over in an instant, but it lasts for an eternity. If you are lucky, you see it coming. If you are even more fortunate, the bear gave you ample warning first.

First, let's state right up front, most charges are bluffs and although it may seem like you are being attacked, it is not necessarily an attack at all. It is a display of dominance and aggression. The bear is making a statement to you in his own language. You are being both challenged and warned.

Your response must show two things. You must be both dominant and willing to yield. If you show any of the prey behaviors, a bluff charge can quickly escalate into a real charge. The bear is testing you when he charges. You cannot afford to fail that test. Any signs of weakness and you can end up mauled or worse.

In situations where there is plenty of space between you and the bear you meet, the bear will sometimes warn you before he charges. Often, he will act agitated by swatting the ground or give you a nice side view so you can admire how big he or she is. It is common for the bear to make huffing noises, growl or drool. This is all about a stressed out bear trying to talk with you. He wants you to know he is feeling disturbed and he is giving you fair warning.

 The charge is also a challenge. Your response is going to determine whether it's all talk and no show, or if you need to be put in your place. When a bear charges you, he is going to come so close to you, he may kick a little dirt on you when he turns or veers away. There is no way to explain how terrifying this is going to be for you. This is why you need to program yourself to do the correct responses. Your mind might go blank, but if you have practiced and your subconscious knows what to do, you will do it! The survival instinct in humans can still function when all else fails. Have faith that you have been designed to live through almost anything, and with the proper training you will!

If you are charged and you stand there paralyzed with fear, this is sort of a neutral response from the bear's point of view. He may accept with good grace your dominant statement of standing your ground. He may opt to yield to you by leaving the scene. So, the good news is, doing nothing but freezing in terror often has good results! So if this is the minimum response you can muster, go for it. Just don't allow yourself to indulge in screaming or fleeing. This can actually trigger the predator/prey response in the bear. Instead of turning away, he may take you down or give chase. This is not a good situation to be in. Stand your ground, keep your shouts in a loud, deep tone, take slow, steady breaths.

If you want to increase your odds for successfully standing down a charge, the bear dance is the best way to hedge your bets. Add a bear horn to the equation to befuddle the bear and you have almost a fool-proof response to a charge. Everything you can do to stack the odds in your favor will add to your survival potential during this perilous situation. Add bear spray to the equation and you can hedge this bet to an almost sure thing.

Dancing a Charge

The bear dance in response to a charge has worked for me as a stand-alone response, at least one time. In the situation I am referring to I had absolutely no bear defense implements on me when I tested this theory. Inadvertently, of course! I never meant to deliberately tempt fate and the charge happened when I was unprepared. I did the best I could with what I had, which was nothing!

The charge occurred when I accidently startled a bear who was fishing. I was about 30 feet away from this mid-sized brownie when she blasted out of the stream at me with no preliminary warnings. I danced and yelled HAY!!! I stood my ground in terrified horror and she turned away at the last possible moment. Just a few feet away! Then she casually trotted back into the river, glancing back in my direction with her ears pinned back. The message was obvious, she was trying to feed herself and I had rudely interrupted her. I didn't wait around for round two. I did some thigh slapping as I backed way a few steps and then I stood there with my hands on my hips for a moment to catch my breath. I was so scared, I was practically having a coronary. She resumed her fishing. I retreated dancing until out of sight. I was a nervous wreck until I got home. I was queasy, clammy, and shaking like an aspen in a hurricane. To this day, I blame some of my grey hairs on this bear. But she taught me a very important lesson. You have to hold it together. No matter how stressful or terrifying the situation is, choose to live through it!

We have already talked about the bear dance, but let's review. You shout at the bear in your deepest voice. You clap your hands and slowly wave an arm. Next, stomp your foot and slap your thigh loudly, in no particular order. You are in "bear speak" saying, you are the dominant bear. This totally gets a bear's attention, because by now he is pretty sure you are *not* a bear. You would think that acting challenging toward a bear would get you in a lot of trouble. Strangely enough, they seem to respect you for it and often leave. This is how bears communicate, negotiate, and operate. Halleluiah!

Advancing a Charge

There is also another tactic you can try if you have the nerve. Try advancing several steps towards the bear while you're doing the bear dance. I make sure to clap my hands and stomp my feet when I advance. This usually befuddles a bear. Nothing he wants to eat ever advances on him. It is a very bold and very challenging move to make. This takes huge amounts of courage and it seems insane, but it can cut short all his posturing and bluffing. It can also turn a charge in progress away from you before he gets too close. It is very counter intuitive to behave this way around an agitated bear who is being challenging, but it quite often works. It all depends on what is at stake for the bear. (Not recommended for beginners.)

If he is defending a kill, a cache, or a food resource, there is more for him to lose. This wouldn't be the best circumstance in which to try this tactic. The same goes for a mama bear defending cubs too. If a bear acts agitated, bluff charges you, and remains in the area without yielding, you will need to get out of there ASAP! Assume he is defending something precious whether you can see it or not. Bears don't always like to share. Dance away, but keep an eye on him in case he pulls something else.

The best time to use an advancing reply to a charge is with a lone black bear, because they are more easily intimidated. See my other book for some cheap thrills in that department...

Chapter 3   RECREATING SAFELY
                IN BEAR COUNTRY

The Deterrents

There is a lot of stuff out there to alert bears to your presence, or to deter them from getting too "up close and personal."

Many of my closest encounters have occurred with habituated bears. These are bears who are accustomed to humans to one extent or another. I have inadvertently gotten within inches of bears who knew me, no harm done.

Some of my longest encounters have occurred with wild bears. These are almost never close encounters, but if they are far enough away from you to feel safe, they will often linger in the area to check you out. They might blatantly observe you, or they can be very coy and nonchalant about it. Always be careful when any bear acts overly casual or comfortable in your presence. This can have predatory overtones.

Hey Bear!

Let's start with the simplest of all sounds used to alert bears to your presence. Your voice. One of the easiest and most effective deterrents is to shout or call out every few minutes. You should use a nice deep voice. I like to say "Hey Yogi!" but you can say anything you want. You are simply trying to let bears know you're coming. I am vigilant about using a warning shout anytime I am in brushy country or using trails with lots of blind curves or turns. The idea is to *not* surprise a bear at close range. If you bump into a bear in a heavily brushed area, he may feel both surprised and trapped. The defensive response is going to happen so fast you will not have enough time to protect yourself properly. Not a good situation, for him or you. People with small or high pitched voices, or those prone to tender vocal cords, can consider some other options.

Stick Snapping, DON'T!

It has been theorized that one of the most effective bear alerts is to walk along, occasionally snapping a stick. I would have to disagree. This does communicate to a bear he is not alone. And it is usually true they will move out of your way. But this is only because bears are normally of a non-confrontational nature. But what about bears during the mating season? Bears seek other bears during the spring time, and the snapping of a stick might really interest them then. Bears are also very curious and intelligent. Some may approach you to investigate the sound. Other large game animals such as moose are going to snap sticks as they move. This would be of great interest to bears. Walking along snapping sticks is the sort of repetitious behavior I would soon find annoying. Finding a supply of sticks might be problematic too, depending on where you are hiking. It's an interesting theory, but I'm not sold on the idea at all.

Sing those Bears Away

Another recommendation is to sing. I don't mind doing a little singing if no one is around or in danger of hearing me. But for bears, it doesn't work. On three different occasions I had my singing interrupted by some big brownie cubs coming at me full blast. Apparently they ran down out of the hills to investigate the dying animal sounds. Yeah, it's obvious to me and anyone who's heard me, I sound like a hyena with its tail slammed in the door. People like me shouldn't even sing in the shower. I don't want to be party pooper though. Give singing a try. Especially if you have a deep, resonant voice. If you are a soprano, you might want to think twice. High-pitched sounds are the song of the dead and the dying in the animal kingdom. You might think you sound great, but what would a bear think?

Bear Bells

Bear bells can really backfire on you too. It is true, they will alert bears in the area to your presence and it is always a good thing to avoid surprising a bear. A good place to use them would be in a heavy brush, or in any low visibility situation. However, there is good anecdotal evidence bear bells sometimes attract curious bears not familiar with them. Remember, bears love to investigate any really interesting sound. Attracting a curious bear might be counter-productive if you truly don't want to see a bear. But the biggest factor is, once again, the annoyance. Walking behind someone who is clanging or tinkling steadily is very irritating. A few miles of this torture and I am ready to maul them myself! I am out there to be a part of nature. I love to listen to the birds singing and the brooks babbling. Furthermore, I love to see bears, though preferably at a distance, because they always add excitement to a hike. Once again, you may feel very differently, so act accordingly. Remember the old joke: How can you tell brown bear scat from black bear scat? The brown bear scat contains lots of bells. Love that sick humor...

My best use for bear bells is when I'm camping in black bear country. I will attach them to my food bag to let me know if I am the recipient of an uninvited guest. If I hear the jingling of bells off in the distance, it might mean I'm about to go on a diet. Oh well, it hasn't happened yet.

Spray Them Away

Bear spray is very popular in the world of commercial bear deterrents. It is made of capsicum, derived from cayenne peppers, hence it's name - pepper spray. This is mixed into an oil base along with some high pressure propellants. Different brands claim different distances the spray can reach, but it is usually about twenty to thirty feet. These products have been in use long enough to produce favorable data to support carrying them. Some of the best reasons to consider pepper spray is that it is compact and light weight. It can be situated in a holster for a quick draw. All good!

Statistics show it is reasonably effective when used properly. It works by causing stinging and discomfort in the bear's eyes and respiratory passages. This means you have to hit the bear in the face with it, or it won't work. It won't bother him a bit if you hose his furry body down with gallons of it.

Bear spray can put a human out of commission for twenty to thirty minutes. It is only going to be uncomfortable for a bear for about ten minutes, assuming you get a direct hit. You should use that time to get as far away as possible!

The Downside of Pepper Spray

Some of the drawbacks include; possible blow back upon yourself if you are using it in the wind, or even if it is completely still. If you get even the tiniest bit of mist upon your face, you will end up in a world of hurt, hardly able to see anything. This is not a good idea during a close encounter situation, but it is a probable result. The smallest of back-drafts can send you into coughing fits where you will be gasping for breath. This is a blatant prey behavior and puts you in a perilous situation on many levels. Bears are much more tolerant of bear spray than people are. Using bear spray is inherently risky.

There can be an accidental discharge upon unexpected impacts, or when it is being used by someone who is uncertain or inexperienced. There have been folks who have been too shaky to release the trigger guard, so can't fire it in a stressed encounter, bummer!

Lack of range is another issue. The bear has to be in your personal space before you can use it. (20 to 30 feet away) It is much better to back off dancing than to wait for a bear to get close enough to have to use it.

Because it is only going to last for 4 to 6 seconds, it is easy to run out of spray while trying to get it in his face. Many people panic and start blasting away before a bear is close enough to be affected. They are running on empty when he actually arrives. That sucks.

Another problem is that bears seem to like the taste of it. They will lick it off things it has been discharged on. It is ironic that once discharged, pepper spray might be an attractant! So if you use it in an area where you are camping, you will need to relocate to a fresh spot. If it is all over your gear, good luck with that!

Many people haven't got a clue how to use bear spray and few bother to train and practice deployment in advance. Alaska legend insists that there have been people who think it is a repellent and have sprayed themselves with it instead of the bear! I guess that is a mistake you would only make once.

When being transported by "bush planes" it is a serious concern. An accidental deployment caused by the shifting of cargo could be potentially fatal. Many bush pilots don't like to transport the stuff unless it is contained in something designed to withstand an accidental dispersal. You, for sure, cannot take it on any commercial flights even in checked baggage, so you must purchase it after you land at your destination.

An accidental deployment in a small backpackers tent could be potentially fatal too. You won't be able to see the zipper to escape. Being forced to inhale significant amounts of it could cause such inflamed airways you may have trouble breathing at all.

It is a hazardous material so it must be shipped by ground via truck or boat, and it is inconvenient to obtain. It is also about $30.00 to $60.00 a canister to purchase, so it is a significant expense. It has a shelf life and needs to be shaken frequently to keep everything in suspension. Old canisters should be used to practice with, but costs usually are too prohibitive to practice with new spray. If people haven't practiced deploying the spray properly, (in short bursts) they might actually run out of spray before the bear gets close enough to hit them with it. That leaves them in big trouble if spray was all they had with them. Don't let bear spray be your only line of defense. But if you are going to carry it, I strongly recommend you take some training in how to use it properly. The time to read the instructions for the first time is not when you have a bear standing in front of you.

Precipitation is also going to be a problem, the spray works very poorly in a downpour. Having lived in the rain forest most of my life, this is very bad news. Once again, I strongly suggest you have other means to discourage bears besides spray alone. It is too hazardous and not reliable enough to use as a stand-alone deterrent. In fact, never rely on any one thing as your sole means of protection.

Last but not least, there can be problems with the propellants in extreme cold or hot temperatures.

Carry it Anyway

With that sort of a down side, do I carry it? Yes, I usually do. And yes, I have been trained by the US Forest Service in how to safely use it. I have never had to use bear spray on a real bear, but I would like to keep that option open. I depend on other deterrents for my primary defense, but you should always have two or more different deterrents with you at all times. Bear spray can be one of them. Always have a back-up system to go to.

Tase Them

The Department of Fish and Game has been experimenting with the use of Tasers for deterring both moose and bears. The first time it is used on an animal they tend to leave the scene immediately. With bears, they will sometimes return, however.

If used repeatedly over time, some habituated bears have developed more of an aversion to people. This can be a good thing if they have been getting themselves into trouble eating garbage and such. It may become a valuable tool to change behavior. Not in one lesson, but slowly over time.

It seems that tasing a bear is less stressful to the animal than darting it. It looks like Tasers may become a useful option as a non-lethal deterrent in some situations.

The type of Taser used is the high powered MX26, which is stronger than the model designed for use on people. Penetrating the thick coat of a bear can be an issue. It shoots a barbed hook on a tether. The smaller the bear, the better it seems to work. I spoke with one

Officer who tased a black bear from the safety of his cruiser. The bear fell down, then leaped to his feet and bolted away. Stay tuned, there are some interesting possibilities here.

Burn Bear, Burn!

Some people carry flares with them for protection. Flares are another interesting idea that should work, at least in theory. They might be useful when defending a campsite at night. There are road flares, marine flares, gun-fired flares, and assorted firework options.

There are some drawbacks to flares, explosives, and all things which burn and go bang. First and foremost, they are tricky to use. You have to light them, load them or hit them. They are subject to accidental activation. They are difficult to carry, activate and store. And yep, you can't hide them on an airplane either. Last but not least, there are always those pesky things which can be accidently lit on fire. Like your tent, or the forest you are camping in. We don't worry much about these things in our rainy climate, but you might have to.

Tingle That Bear

There are lots of other possibilities for those camping out. An electric fence around your campsite can be very effective. An inquisitive bear who is exploring around your camp can get a little snap on his wet nose. This will send most bears running for the hills. They don't seem to realize they could knock it all down with very little effort. However, the ones who don't touch the fence with their nose first, do sometimes knock them down. So, this isn't entirely foolproof. It all depends on the sturdiness of the structure and the strength of the current flowing through it.

Electric fences are a little cumbersome for backpackers, but I used to utilize one when I was camping out with our kids. It was hard to properly ground the fence on some of the dry beaches we stayed at. They are also a bit of a hassle to set up and take down, too.

The biggest problem with the fence was that our children couldn't leave the thing alone. They would sit there by the hour like drooling idiots, repeatedly shocking themselves and daring each other to lick the wire. They put a serious drain on the battery by the time we needed to bed down. I never did know if there was enough juice left in the thing to give a bear a good tingle or not.

It is of interest to note that good quality electric fences are sometimes used in official camping areas in bear country. The US Forest Service provides portable fences to some of their crews living out in the back country. I have a friend who used one to keep her horses safe. You will see how that was done in the last chapter.

Put the "Moves" on Them

How about the "CritterGitter" motion detector? This is very clever motion sensor technology that sounds a loud alarm when triggered. But of course, it is not without some drawbacks. First, any significant motion will set it off. It could be any animal wandering by. Or it might be a person who has to sneak out of your tent to take a pee. It doesn't matter what it is. One false alarm will get the adrenaline pumping if you are out camping. Once you have been scared out of your wits by a squirrel, it sure is hard to get back to sleep. Still, it is an idea with many merits and the alarm itself is startling enough to scare a bear away. (At least temporarily.) There is a lot of logic in using loud and strange noises to freak out bears. I think this one deserves some serious consideration, as well as other companies that provide this technology.

Bang That Bad Boy

How about Bird Bangers and Bear Bangers? They make these non-lethal bear guns in Canada and they really are called "Bear Bangers." They shoot a shotgun-like shell which goes off with a bang when fired, then makes a second bang when it's about fifty yards out. The same goes for the birds. The Bird Banger shells can actually be fired from a regular 12 gauge shotgun and I like to keep one in my barrel when I am on bear duty. I figure it is better to have a non-lethal round in the chamber for both a warning shot and as a safety round in case of an accidental discharge.

It is another interesting idea, but there are some potential drawbacks. What if the wad goes past the bear, then goes bang behind them? This could startle the bear into running towards you instead of away. Oops! Anything which sounds like a gun, can be a problem too, read on...

Shoot em Up!

Let's talk about firearms. At first glance, they seem like a great idea. In the hands of a skilled shooter with nerves of steel, it could be the decisive factor in saving your life if you are truly being attacked. The odds of you actually being the victim of a predatory encounter are astronomical, but it does happen.

(Please keep in mind, being charged by a bear is not the same as being attacked in a predatory mode.) A charge is a act of dominance from a stressed out challenger, nothing more, nothing less, unless you respond inappropriately.

If a bear is coming at you silently, eyes locked on you and ears up, you are in serious trouble, because these are potentially predatory behaviors. This bear is either a very habituated bear who is being way too friendly, or it is a bear who seriously sees you as a potential meal. Using a gun to defend yourself in a predatory situation is appropriate. Using guns in other situations is not an appropriate *first* response.

If you have an agitated bear posturing, swatting the ground, huffing, snapping his jaws and frothing at the mouth, the bear is stressed out and is simply trying to sort out some dominance issues or defend something. The good news is, they probably don't want eat you for dinner. There is no reason to shoot this bear other than your own fear, but sadly, nearly all the bears getting themselves shot were just posturing and nothing more. They can usually be dealt with by doing a dancing retreat.

I usually only pack my shotgun when I am going to be camped out with people, or I am involved with a very long, off the trail trek. Consequently, I have never actually had a gun in my possession when I've been charged, so I have never made the mistake of shooting a stressed-out bear simply acting out. I have been forced to handle charges without the benefit of a firearm to back me up. So, I have had to be creative.

The interesting thing about aggressive-appearing bear behaviors is that you are in the most amount of danger when the bear looks the least angry, as in the "predatory mode." The bear who is putting on the aggressive act is terrifying in his actions, but is really just playing games with you or trying to deliver a warning. The bluff charge is part of this mentality and he can do it repeatedly without ever touching you. It is a terrifying experience, but you will probably live to tell about it if you don't do anything too stupid, like screaming, running or playing dead. Try not to shoot in this situation because wounding an agitated bear will possibly get you killed. A bear who is just bluffing and gets shot, won't be bluffing any more. You may be toast if you don't kill him right then and there. So, using a gun can escalate a merely terrifying situation into a lethal event, maybe the bear, maybe you. Don't be in a hurry to shoot a bear just because you interpret his behavior as aggressive or frightening. But do get the heck out of their using the dominant retreat. (dance)

The Big Bang Theory

Now, having said all this, let's talk about those who do decide to shoot a bear because it has charged them or because they have surprised one in a tight situation. For starters, dropping a bear who is running at you at thirty miles an hour is harder than you would think. Even a huge bear doesn't present a very large target with its head down facing you straight on and coming at you like a bull. If the charge occurs at close range, you will be lucky to be able to raise a gun up and aim it, let alone get an accurate shot off. You might actually be better off smacking the bear with the gun if an encounter gets this close!

If you are charged from a distance you have more time, but it is a difficult shot, regardless. If a bear is bluff charging and you shoot him, all bets are off. They may keep on coming because you have hurt them. Bears take it very personally when you shoot them. Usually it inspires rage. But the facts of the matter are, it often takes multiple shots to drop a bear on the run, even with an elephant gun. An enraged bear can take a lot of lead before it succumbs. There is good statistical evidence that more people are injured or killed when shooting a bear, than are those who are only using bear spray in self-defense. It can be done, but it is far from a sure thing and a wounded bear is a very dangerous bear.

Once again, some more sick bear humor to break up the tension: One guy asks his friend if the gun he is carrying is big enough to kill a bear? There are two possible replies here. The other guy says, "I don't have to shoot the bear, I just need to shoot you, so I can outrun him." The other possible reply is; "I don't need to

shoot the bear, I just need to shoot myself."
Tee hee.

Dinners On!

Then, there are bears who are turned on by gun-fire. Yep, you heard me right. It gets them very excited. These are usually bears living in areas frequented by hunters. They have learned that a gunshot is the same thing as ringing the dinner bell. If they come running, they will be rewarded with a nice big gut pile to snack on, especially if they are the first one on the scene.

Shooting in the air around one of these bears is certainly not going to scare them away. In fact they will get turned on and hungry instead, not a good thing for you. I have many friends who are subsistence hunters in Alaska. In some areas, as soon as the deer or moose is down, it's a race to see if you can gut your game and drag it away before the bears show up for their reward. Gun fire only means, "dinner's on," to these bears.

In my own personal experience, I have tried firing a gun into the air or into the ground to get bears to back off when in a "Mexican standoff." I have had very little response from some habituated bears. You would think it would bother their sensitive hearing, but bears can easily tolerate loud noises of short duration, especially at a distance of twenty or thirty feet.

Even a wild bear will dependably, only run once after you fire a warning shot. He might be right back because curiosity often overrides caution. If the big bang was scary, but of no actual harm, why not go back and see why? A shot in the air might work and it might not. You should always change your location, once you have tried this tactic. Don't be waiting for them if they decide to come back. Get yourself gone.

Rubber Bullets, Oh my!

We did some experimentation with rubber bullets out at Kitoi Bay Hatchery in an attempt to try to deter bears away from the hatchery barrier nets. At a nice safe distance, my husband Tim, rump shot a couple of bears while they were playing with the forbidden nets. Each gave a startle reaction upon impact, but didn't run. A couple shots later they were slowly moving out of the area while giving us dirty looks.

The next day they were back again and we repeated the experiment. This time the bears barely flinched and went right on with their business. They gave us the occasional evil look, but wouldn't budge. So much for rubber bullets. We weren't impressed and neither were they. Maybe a little black bear would be intimidated, but not our big brownies.

A Gun, and Only a Gun? NO!

My recommendation would be to only have one gun bearer for a group of people. The firearm should be handled only by a person well trained for the job and who has a lot of practice and experience with firearms. This person needs to understand bear behavior and mannerism and most importantly, must have nerves of steel and good judgment. They need to be smart enough to know when *not* to shoot. Few people fit this profile and everyone needs to recognize this. Guns in the hands of fools have some very sorry outcomes in bear country.

If you are the designated gun bearer, carry a big one. Leave those 357s and 45s at home, they do not have enough stopping power. I prefer a 12 guage shotgun because I have no intention of shooting a bear unless he is right in front of me. Use a front carry tactical sling which keeps the weapon in your hands and in the ready position at all times. It can be fired in a pinch while still connected to the carrying harness. Or the quick release can be used if you have more time. Even better, you can let go of the gun to grab your horn or bear spray as a more practical first option. The gun will still be waiting for you in ready position if you need to use it. Yes, the gun bearer needs to carry the other deterrents too. A firearm is only very rarely needed.

The gun I use is has a stainless steel barrel and a folding stock with combat grips. I usually have a bird banger in the barrel and a full load of rifled Brennecke slugs behind that, safety on. It is always with me on my front mount tactical sling unless I am sleeping. Then it is in easy reach above my head.

I don't always carry a gun, especially if I am backpacking and weight is a consideration. But even for backpacking, this rig works. The front carry position does not interfere with backpacking equipment and it helps balance the load.

A gun in a scabbard or a backpack is totally useless in a tight situation. Don't even bother with it. It's just dead weight to haul around like you're going to be if you surprise the wrong bear.

I have a lot to say about guns. When I was sweet, young, and single, I never carried guns of any sort. I figured it was only me and the world wouldn't suffer because there was one less idiot. When I got married and had a couple cubs of my own, my view changed completely. I became a very defensive mama bear myself, yet I have never had to shoot a bear. The biggest challenge of swaggering around with a gun, is knowing when *not* to use it. I want to state for the record, I do not recommend carrying a gun as your sole source of protection. It can be a part of your arsenal, but you should be carrying a horn and pepper spray too. Having several different response options at your disposal is always the safest bet.

Blow That Bear Away!

Well, you might be getting the idea there is nothing out there which works every time for every bear, and you might be right. But this brings us to my favorite bear deterrent, the horn.

I first started to use a marine safety horn with both our habituated and wild Afognak Island bears. The first time I used it on either type of bear at close range it would send them running. The bears who lived with us on a routine basis however, quickly became accustomed to my horn and very non-reactive the next time I used it. This didn't discourage me. I used it anyway, especially if they were too close to me for any reason. Just because a bear does not respond immediately, doesn't mean it is not working. Sometimes I would use a horn on a non-reactive habituated bear by blowing the horn continually until they back down. Sooner or later, the bear would start shaking its head and back away or exit the scene. The horn hurts their ears at close range and was at least annoying to them a little farther out. But, most important, it never seemed to induce reprisals.

Like all things, the horn has some serious limitations. When I first started carrying a horn, I used the kind which is gas propelled. Once, after hiking around all summer, I made the very surprising discovery that my horn had lost its charge even though it hadn't been used. Since I made this unfortunate finding when I was in the middle of a close encounter, it made quite an impression on me. From that day forward I was never able to trust this kind of a horn again. I found a really loud marine safety horn to take its place. You could blow it using your very own lungs. It possessed a side blow hole, so I modified it with a custom mouth-piece so I could clench the horn in my teeth. This frees up both my hands to grab bear spray or a gun. Also, this modification allows me to find the right place to blow when in a dark tent. I have carried this type of horn ever since.

But let's get back to limitations. A horn blown when a bear is way off in the distance is going to be useless. By the time the bear gets to you, it will have figured out the horn is just a noise. <u>*Don't* use a horn on any bear unless he is in your personal space.</u> The horn only has about the same range as bear spray, no more than twenty to thirty feet around you. The trick with using the horn effectively is not to use it at all until the last possible moment. He should be almost on me, literally right in my face! Then a loud and prolonged toot is all it takes to turn him away. It works very effectively during a full on charge at top speed, but wait for him to arrive! This obviously requires some steady nerves and some discipline. I have successfully turned three Kodiak brown bear charges using only a horn and some dancing.

I always wear my horn on a lanyard around my neck. I am able to have it to my lips and blowing quicker than most people can raise a gun. A horn can be good in close situations when there isn't time for anything else, such as surprising a bear. I don't want to give you the impression that a horn is the only thing I carry, but, along with the bear dance, it is my primary defense. I always carry a minimum of two or three deterrents with me at all times. I often add bear spray and/or a gun also, depending on the situation.

Not just any horn will do either. It needs to have a big, loud, deep sound. Do not be cheap and get one of these smaller, high pitched horns. Bigger is better. A friend demonstrated one which sounded like a deer bleating, not good! Get a big bad horn. It should sound something like a sixteen wheeler truck horn. It should have enough decibels to be piercing and painful up close. If you don't cringe when you blow it, it isn't loud enough. If the horn you select has a side blow hole, be sure to attach a piece of tubing around it to form a mouthpiece. Side holes can't be found in the dark of a tent and force you to use a hand to hold the horn to your lips. You cannot afford these limitations. One of the downfalls of a lung-driven horn is that some people hyperventilate badly during a bear encounter. They might be too breathless for a good blast. If you are this sort of person, perhaps the gas-driven horn is a better model for you. If you use this type, practice using it one handed. Keep your dominant hand available to reach for the bear spray.

Chapter 4   SHARING THE GREAT

OUTDOORS

Sleeping Outside in Bear Country

Most people who read books like this are already well aware you do not keep your food or any scented item in camp with you. They should be safely stowed well away from your campsite. How far? As far away as you would be comfortable seeing a bear from your camp, and this is a different distance for different people.

When I am camping with friends and loved ones, I am heavily armed now. Would I shoot a bear who stops to sniff at my camp? No, of course not, this happens all the time. I will shoot a bear who tries to claw its way into my tent though. And it is very nice to be in a tent strong enough to withstand the initial onslaught of a" bear pounce."

Bears who visit your campsite during the night usually do a little exploring then move right along. I have had them snuffle my tent on several occasions. I have awakened on countless mornings to discover the footprints of bears who have strolled around the tent even when I have not heard them. All of these behaviors are nothing more than intelligent curiosity and do not warrant gun fire or paranoia. If this scenario sounds too frightening to deal with, you belong safe at home, not out in the wilderness where the bears live. There is absolutely no justification for shooting a bear just because they are checking out your campsite.

Bears in Your Camp

If they hang around or start trying to get into your tent, this is another matter. You are going to need to exit any small tent in this situation so you can defend yourself. Remaining in a small tent with an aggressive bear hanging around can be fatal. The problem is being able to tell a predatory bear from a curious bear. First, let's assume you are an intelligent outdoorsman and there are no scented or food items at your campsite.

A curious bear visits you briefly, then leaves. Sometimes this bear will huff quietly because your presence is stressing them a little. It is a frightening situation, but no one gets hurt. Wait it out.

A predatory bear is a bear that won't leave. He won't make a sound. If you manage to scare him off with your bear deterrents, he will come right back, silently, maybe from a different direction. You are in very serious danger with this bear. If you have a gun, be prepared to use it. A big sturdy tent might afford you the option to shoot your way out if the bear starts clawing his way in. This has to be a pounce-proof shelter though. Otherwise, get yourself out into an open area so you can see them coming. Be prepared to spend the night defending yourself with whatever you have. Never give up. This advice is based on surviving a predatory situation of this type. Sorry, see my other book.

Rare Predatory Fatalities and Tent Selection

There was a very sad story about a couple of Alaskans whose outdoor adventure ended in tragedy. They were behaving themselves and doing everything right, but they ended up being eaten by a bear anyway. The actual events happened years ago and involved a couple on a float trip. These were very savvy outdoorsmen who knew exactly how to behave in bear country. They had been making their way down a river for several days without incidence. They had been camping in a small tent and storing their food well away from their tent. They were following all the rules.

One night while they slept, a bear in predatory mode came into their camp. We can only guess at exactly what happened, but it looks like the bear pounced the tent and collapsed it on them. This is easy to do with a small, flimsy, lightweight tent. You become an instant "bear burrito." Even if you are sleeping with a gun in your hand, you would not be able to use it. Sadly, the couple was found in a partially-devoured state, their tent in tatters around them.

It is the kind of story which really makes the headlines, even though it represents a very rare event. What can we learn from this story? Many will simply conclude it is right to fear bears. But we can gain very important knowledge from this tragedy. Namely, that small backpacker tents and the like are not a good idea for camping in when visiting bear country. One little pounce and you can end up wrapped and trapped in the very tent that was supposed to protect you. It would be very natural to scream under the circumstances. With a bear locked into the predator mode, it seals the deal for you. It's all over.

After my own predatory event in a small backpackers tent occurred, endangering the life of my son and myself, I had to rethink my camping strategies. The first rule has to be; no more flimsy little tents. Especially in brown bear habitat. Being a prolific backpacker, I was forced to make some serious changes in my choice of equipment.

Safer Tents

A tent which has a floor in it presents a hazard in bear country. If your tent has been collapsed on you, it makes it impossible to escape. Small solo tents and "only enough room to sit up in" backpacker tents are the worst. What does this leave you with if you want to hike or backpack? You've got to go minimalist with nothing more than a tarp overhead, or with something sturdy, free-standing, and too tall to collapse easily with one pounce.

For backpacking in the Alaskan outback, I use a floorless Kifaru teepee with a seven foot center. It sets up so tautly, that a bear would actually have to claw its way through it to get to you. It would be difficult, but not impossible to knock over. If this does happen, you still might be able to get out since there is no attached floor. Possibly, you could pull some pegs and roll out. The Kifaru is not bear-proof by any stretch of the imagination. Nothing is. But it is designed in such a way that you will have the time you need to awaken and respond to a bear trying to claw his way in. If you are properly armed you have a good chance of surviving a predatory attack, even in the middle of the night. Kifarus are very light. You can sleep four to six people for about seven pounds of carry weight. Add a few more pounds if you want a cozy wood stove to heat it with. It is amazing to bed down in a warm tent which is back packable and relatively secure. They are pricey, but well worth the money for camping in Kodiak brown bear country.

When I am backpacking in the lower 48 in black bear country I simply play the odds. I am not willing to sleep in a floorless tent with bugs, snakes, scorpions etc. I use an ultra-light tent and camp very cleanly. I am not so nervous around black bears as I am around brownies. Hopefully this won't be my downfall. This is one of those do as I say, not as I do situations. I also like skydiving, but I wouldn't recommend it.

A big wall tent with a metal frame is nice choice for long term camping situations, but way too heavy for anything else. There are Weather Ports, Yurts and other beefy temporary structures that will slow a bear down. Remember, there really isn't much of anything that's truly bear proof. But it doesn't need to be bear-proof. You only need to slow them down long enough to defend yourself.

Whistles

Every hiker or backpacker should carry a whistle for safety reasons. They are essential for signaling for help if you should become lost or hurt. I do not recommend the whistle be used as a sound deterrent for bears however. Nor should it be used as a warning to alert bears to your presence. Whistles are too high pitched and might be interpreted by the bear as a prey sound, or maybe something novel that inspires an investigation. Carry them, but don't depend on them to call out a warning for bears in the area.

Alaskan Emergency Food Storage
and Base Camps

When I set up a base camp, or plan to return to a drop off or pick up point, I usually stash an emergency food cache. This often consists of a five gallon bucket containing only canned goods. It is tightly sealed, then hoisted up in a tree or buried. This system is heavy and bulky. There is no intention of hauling it anywhere, it stays in one place. It serves as a back-up system only for emergencies. I have never had this sort of a food cache violated. It works beautifully in the remote areas of Alaska.

Backpacking Food Storage Options

I love to backpack, but I have chosen to ignore bear-vault type food storage containers and the like. I find them too bulky, too heavy, and a major pain in the butt. If you got them, use them. I'm just stating a personal preference here. Unfortunately, there are some National Parks and other areas in the USA where you are forced to use these products. I consider this sort of policy to be a little misguided, but you should always follow the rules in the area you are visiting.

Ursacks

I prefer to use Ursacks for backpacking whenever I can. They are made out of bullet proof cloth and resemble a stuff sack. You can get a lot in them. They crunch down nicely into a backpack, easily conforming to the shape of its contents. Or, they can be lashed to the outside. They are much lighter than the competition's "vault." Everything I put in them gets double zip locked. There is also an inner bag available which seals tightly around your double bagged contents. This really tones down food scents. This is a really good idea to do regardless of the food storage system you decide to use.

Another trick to reducing odor is simply packing bland foods. Leave that pepperoni and smoked fish at home. Be sensible in your food choices. Use those multiple layers of sealed zip-lock bags. At night, I situate my Ursacks in a backdrop of other powerful scents. If you can, choose an area with strong smells, like flowers, skunk cabbage, or pungent brush. You get the idea. Tie your sack securely with the recommended figure eight knot. There is no hoisting, no burying, no hassles. I have never had my Ursack disturbed, even when bears are all around me.

Be sure to store all your cosmetics, soap, toothpaste, deodorants, bug spray, chewing gum, garbage, cooking pots or anything with a scent the same way. In my kit, I use at least two Ursacks. A big one for all my food items and a smaller one for everything else which has a scent for this duty. I usually opt for the lighter, rodent proof version for my cosmetics and extras. It works for me and I appreciate the lighter weight and pack ability this system has to offer. Is it bear proof? No, but nothing really is. Get over it! It keeps the rodents out and they are a worse problem than bears are in many areas.

Storing Perishable Food Items
when Camping in Remote Areas

Another method of food storage I use when I am camping out is Coleman coolers and the like. I am referring to the big, sturdy, plastic coolers you can buy anywhere. I load them with my perishables. By light of day they are in my food preparation area, which is always separate from my camping/sleeping area. At dusk, I haul them off to yet a different location before I bed down for the night. I place several wraps of duct tape completely around the cooler, covering the latch, or latches. Then, I just leave it sitting there well away from game trails, water sources or any place that would attract any furry foot traffic. When I am on the coast, I will set the cooler on a high pinnacle of rock if there is one handy.

Bears are masterful at opening things so this is far from a sure thing. But this system has been 100% successful for me thus far. I have never had a cooler violated yet. This sort of thing would be questionable or illegal in some areas, so check with the local authorities before you try this. It is an economical and reasonable food storage system to try in remote areas. Again, please don't do this in popular camping areas where it could endanger others. Store your food in the proper receptacles.

Chapter 5   LIVING IN BEAR COUNTRY

Bear Attractants in your Own Backyard

People are often surprised to learn about the interests they might inadvertently share with bears. Many people enjoy bird watching and take special pleasure in observing the shenanigans that go on at the feeders in their own backyards. Bears also take pleasure in the delights offered at your feathered friend's favorite stop too, especially when it is brimming with your generous donations. Bears find bird cuisine of all sorts enticing and delicious, be it seed or suet, and will go to great lengths to empty out your kind contributions. The same can be said for garbage, barbeques, bee hives, orchards and gardens. Bears and people have many passions in common and this can lead to problems.

When living in bear country you are going to have to ask yourself some very serious questions about the attractants you possess that bears find so irresistible. This is a very complex issue which not only involves you, but your neighbors. Inadvertently inviting bears to your property is a community affair that affects everyone. Bears aren't a welcome sight on your property when you or your neighbors have children or pets to worry about. What about granny stringing up her laundry out back? People like to feel safe when on their home turf. Hungry bears hanging about looking for mischief is a problem we create with our shared interests.

Since it isn't fair to hold a bear accountable for his or her intention of keeping their tummies full, it is up to us to discourage them from looking to us for a free lunch. A bear's presence on our property is usually something for which we need to take total responsibility for. Let's take a look at a couple of the most common bear attractants to be found in our yards.

Thanks to the internet and all the fabulous pictures on Google Images, we can now plainly see a multitude of pictures of bears visiting back yards everywhere. They love bird feeders and will go to great lengths to get at them. Black bears hanging like acrobats from feeders are quite the spectacle. Often, after they empty out the bird feeders they move on to the grill. They are very happy to lick it all clean for you for your next barbeque. With that task finished, a survey of the leftovers in your trash can be of interest. Once the immediate food needs are taken care of its time for some play. Might as well bat the can around a little and spread the trash about in an artful display. Do you have a swing set or a pool? Anything is fair game for a furry visitor in mischief mode. Might as well see what's on your porch or look in a few windows. Where does a bear draw the line? He doesn't. If you are living in bear country, you are the one responsible for drawing the lines.

Some Surprising Bear Passions

A bear will kill you for a carrot, who knew? Bears have some cravings so intense that they will go to great lengths to satisfy them, and carrots fall into this category. I am going to go out on a limb here and declare the humble, domestic carrot, to possibly be a bears favorite food. Yep, better than salmon, tastier than rancid moose entrails or any of the other meaty delights that a bear enjoys. The common garden variety of carrot is like catnip to a bear. They will roll their eyes in ecstasy and gush puddles of drool at the sight of one. A vegan running around with a knapsack full of carrots could be in mortal peril... I am serious, folks, bears go crazy for them!

Once, I volunteered to take care of a friend's property for the summer. They had a charming cabin in Long Lake, Alaska, and had planted a big, attractive garden that required some tending. Our kids were little and it seemed like a great idea to fly into the Alaskan interior to enjoy this warm paradise for a month. I jumped at the chance to escape our coastal rains.

There was an assortment of inland grizzly that were hanging around the place when we arrived. I thought that was a real bonus being the bear nut that I am. The cabin was near a salmon stream and the bears were starting to get very interested in fishing. I was content to weed and water the huge garden on the premises and didn't mind sharing space with the resident bears. They did their thing and I did mine. I kept the kids close to me, rather than letting them run wild though. I was always amazed that the bears mostly ignored the garden. It was loaded with delicious food that we certainly appreciated, but the bears didn't even seem interested.

Then one day, they discovered the row of carrots residing there. They were about half grown at the time, young and tender. The bears carefully dug up each individual carrot and ate it on the spot. A huge row of them vanished in one mornings work. Everything else was ignored, even so it was a substantial feast. I marveled at the very careful way they harvested these gold nuggets. Not a trace of a carrot left anywhere. I accepted the loss with good grace and humor, after all, bears will be bears.

The next day I was shocked to find that the bears had dug a trench in the garden where the carrots used to be. Apparently they must have thought there were more hiding down below. There weren't. They left a ditch nearly two feet deep and about 20 feet long. Dirt was spread all over the place. It was a mess! I filled the trough back in as best I could. I was very impressed with the amount of work they had done with no return on their investment.

It got even more interesting. The following morning I woke up to find the entire garden destroyed. A sow and her three cubs had trampled all the cabbages into a row of coleslaw. They had torn down the peas, beans and corn. Vegetable corpses were everywhere. It didn't look like they had eaten any of it. Apparently they decided to ransack the entire garden just in case a carrot might have been hidden amongst it. I called the owners to report the bad news. The garden was toast except for a half smashed row of potatoes. But that's not all!

That very night in a fit of angst over the carrot drought, the bears tore up the irrigation system and punched a hole in a nearby green house to gain entry. The damage was starting to get serious. They took to hanging around the cabin and looking in the windows. We had no carrots in our possession, but we were wholly under siege. I called my husband to come and rescue us. The bears had totally lost their minds after the carrot rampage and we decided to make a run for it. Addiction is a terrible thing when it comes to bears!

Organic Gardening

I have always had an interest in growing vegetables. One year I created a lovely raised bed garden at our home at Kitoi Bay on Afognak Island. We had some spoiled fish meal on hand and I decided it would make a nice addition to our rather poor soil. I figured it might be a little risky in bear country, but if I worked a little of it well into the soil, it would decompose very rapidly. I planted my little plot and it really took off. It was mostly lettuce, potatoes, and crucifers. Not much else would grow in this cold, wet, climate. The garden lasted a couple weeks before it was discovered by our local bears. One day I arrived home from a hike to find a mother bear with three cubs busily excavating my plot. They were ignoring the vegetables other than to get them out of the way and toss them to the side. They were actually eating the dirt itself! By now the fish meal was well composted and represented only a small fraction of the soil. They scooped the delicious earth up in ravenous delight. I was shocked at how much they were loading into their mouths. They grinned happily like children slathered in chocolate pudding. When they finished with their work, there was nothing left but a hole in the ground surrounded by trampled seedlings. So using fish or kelp fertilizers is a very bad idea, lesson learned!

Fruits of any Kind

Bears love all fruits and berries. In areas that have a wild abundance of these things, they make them a big part of their diet in the summer and fall. They have no qualms about trying all kinds of fruit that are not found in their natural habitat. This could be your patch of boysenberries or a tree full of cherries or apples. Those with commercial orchards and farms in bear country often take heavy losses from bears eating amazing quantities of fruit as well as the damage of having a bear tearing up bushes and trees as they try and get to the treasures within. As far as I know, electric fences are the only thing that discourage bears from helping themselves, and not even that is a sure thing. Another option I have seen used is for the farmer to set aside an area where the culls and over ripe fruits are set out deliberately for their ursine guests. This can reduce damage to the crop if they don't have to ravage your plants to get adequately fed. Deliberately feeding bears is against the law in most areas however, so this gets a little tricky. On the one hand, you are giving the bears what they will take anyway. But you are also encouraging their presence when you do so.

Bee Hives

A bear's love for honey is legendary, but the problem is that they want everything the hive offers. This includes the bee larvae which are just as appealing. He won't hesitate to dismantle and destroy an entire hive to get the goods. If you want to keep bees, you are going to take your losses if you don't install them in armored or electrified enclosures. Preferably both. Once our furry friends get into bees, they are very difficult to dissuade.

Pet Food, Etc.

No matter what kind of a pet you have, a bear will be interested in trying his food. Dog and cat food is especially attractive to bears. Don't feed your pets outside and don't store their food in vulnerable areas like the porch or mud room. The hay in the barn is enticing, the rabbit pellets, irresistible. Your llama rations could be delightful, and your ostrich chow, alluring. Bears are very open minded in sampling exotic provisions. The same goes for anything a human eats. Bears are willing to try it all.

Oooh, Ick! - Flour Power

I had friends who kept their grub stake in an outdoor shed. They came home to discover they had been robbed. The bear busted down the door and got a 50 lb barrel of flour open. Most of it was eaten! There was a huge mess in their shed to say the least. They got out their guns and decided to track the culprit. It wasn't difficult to do because the bear left a trail of thick, gooey white vomit that was very easy to follow. They found the poor devil laid out in the woods moaning pitifully. They had intended to dispatch him but found his condition so comically pathetic, they decided the belly ache was punishment enough. I was glad to hear they hadn't done him in. It is not the bear's fault when he chooses to pursue a handy food source, it was theirs. There is a good reason most caches in Alaska are usually powerful forts on tall posts, separate from living quarters. A bear can break into almost any house or a cabin that has food in it, if it is undefended. Then the party really gets rolling! Check the internet for tons of hilarious pictures of people's homes being ripped to shreds by bears looking for a good time. Oh those chocolate chip cookies left cooling on the counter, who can blame them?

George Gets Some Company

We had a neighbor once that was cooking some elk for dinner. A very big brownie boar (male) climbed up on his porch to investigate. We immediately phoned George to let him know he had a visitor. George loaded up his hunting rifle and sat down on the far side of his living room from the door. He assured us he would be shooting the bear if he managed to get in and warned us to stay back. We watched the spectacle from the safety of our own kitchen as the bear put his shoulder into the door and leaned heavily into it. The steel door bowed in but held. We were all holding our breath as the drama unfolded. A dog finally ran the bear off, but it sure was a close call for George.

Raising Farm Animals

In Alaska, raising animals is a perilous adventure in bear country. I had a friend that kept horses in a land where bears are quite accustomed to dining on moose and deer. So Gayle used a baited electrical fence. This is a an electrical fence that has a few strongly scented metal bait strips installed on it. In other words, she was deliberately trying to entice bears to her fence for a nice little surprise. She hung these metal strips all around and kept them painted with bacon grease. This would entice the local bears to sniff or lick these electrified bait strips. It really popped them good! The bears became very respectful of her electric fence after being suckered in for a sniff, it totally worked! She had bears breaking into her chicken coop and everywhere else, but they stayed away from her horses. She was able to keep them for many years that way with no problems.

Defense of Life and Property

Once a bear has discovered it is an easy living exploiting human homes and properties, it is very difficult to straighten them out again. Most of these incorrigible bears will end up having to be shot or if they are lucky, relocated. Once again, a fed bear usually does become a dead bear. I can't emphasize enough that it is our responsibility to keep them from going down this sorry path. Don't build your home or cabin near a spawning stream, or in the middle of a blue berry thicket. Respect bear habitat. We are continually encroaching into their home lands and ecosystems, and we act shocked when they return the favor.

Bears are not territorial so they have no innate or natural respect for your home or property either. We are very territorial and defensive of what we believe to be ours, so it is hard for us to grasp an animal that ranges in such a free spirited manner. Bears are opportunists that wander far and wide to keep their bellies full. If it smells good, eat it! If it smells bad, eat it! If it smells weird, at least bite it for good measure. This pretty much sums up the limitations of bear cuisine. There aren't any!

Bears are famous for their perverse sense of culinary entertainment. I had a friend that stashed 6 steel cans of gas deep in the woods to fuel his skiff. He was shocked to find them a week later, dead empty. A bear had carefully bit into each can and let them drain out. You would think a bear would lose interest after biting the first one. But no, the bear went right down the line and tested each one. Bears have bitten many an Avon rubber boat. Not just one chamber, but all of them just for good measure. Air hissing out of puncture wounds is apparently engaging. They have chewed up chest waiters, probably that yummy fish smell intrigued them. In another instance, a bear got in somebody's garage and bit every aerosol can in it. Paint, pesticides, you name it. Perhaps the explosions were a thrill, hard to say what is going through a bears mind when they are amusing themselves at your expense. Nothing is sacred or off limits to a bear. So if you have chosen to reside in bear country, this is what you are up against. Bears will be bears, get over it!

How do we Keep Bears out of our Stuff?

There are two philosophies about how to keep bear out of our belongings. One is to accept the fact that we have interests in common and take your losses gracefully. The problem with this idea is that it only works if you live in an area that is so remote you are not jeopardizing your neighbors. Anytime you allow a bear to ransack your carrots, pick your berries or violate your food stores, you have endangered your neighbors. Once a bear begins to associate a food source with humans, he might jump to the dangerous conclusion that where there are people, there are yummy treats. Your poor unsuspecting neighbor may then be his next visit. This never ends well for the bear or for your neighbors.

Plan two involves defensive strategies. Everything that interests a bear must be heavily barricaded, defended or eliminated. I favor the latter, lead a bear not into temptation, but deliver him from evil - that being you. Don't have anything around that would interest a bear, play it safe. If you feel you must have an orchard or keep animals on your property, be prepared to barricade and defend them. The most effective barrier is a good solid fence or better yet, a complete enclosure that has been electrified.

Old fashioned bear caches like we have in Alaska work too. Because they are high up on stilts, the bear can't get any solid leverage on them to tear them apart.

Other Options

Rubber bullets and the like do not work on big grizzly bears. They are more effective on small bears and black bears, but not a sure thing by any means. Since bears have a way of showing up randomly, it is almost impossible to sit vigil with this kind of a deterrent 24/7.

Bear spray has not been proven to change established bear behaviors either. It can slow a bear down for about ten minutes, then they will be back to lick it off the surroundings. Bears find pepper spray delicious, so that will possibly bring them back for more.

Tasers show promise in reconditioning bears, but they have to be used repeatedly and the Tasers that are strong enough for bears aren't available to the public as far as I know. Once again, this would require weeks of vigilance in retraining the bear and this usually isn't practical.

Karelian bear dogs are bread specifically to deal with bears and other big game. They are a type of aggressive hunting dog that have been used at Yosemite and Glacier National Parks for bear control. I have personally seen them in action and their herding skills are impressive. I had friends who used three dogs to keep their property free of ursine intruders. The downside was that the bears fled to the neighbors property instead. The neighbors weren't that thrilled with the arrangement.

The bottom line is this: you have to prevent a bear from getting into anything they shouldn't be into in the first place. Once they start down the wrong path, it will result in the endangerment of all people residing in or visiting that area, and eventually end in their own probable death. Budgets usually don't allow for live-trapping and relocating bears. Moving a bear from one location to another only results in a bear taking his new bad habits to a fresh location. In Alaska, a number of troubled bears were live-trapped and moved from a bush town out onto a remote island and turned loose. After years of dropping off problem grizzlies there, a population of especially aggressive bears got established. Hiking and camping on that island is thrilling beyond belief!

So, my friends, it is entirely up to you. Since bears aren't likely to behave themselves, you're going to have to. People have always thought they are smarter than bears, it is about time we step up to the plate an prove it. Get educated, act responsibly!

Chapter 6   SUMMARY/ LISTS

1. Be bear aware - always be vigilant in bear country. Look all around you, front, back and sides. Anticipate bear habitat. Berries, fish, water resources? Know where they are likely to be hanging around.

2. Notify - make noise. Loud deep shouts or hand claps every few minutes, especially in brushy areas or trails with blind curves. Never surprise a bear and you will avoid most trouble.

3. Always carry all of your bear deterrents in an instant ready position. It shouldn't take more than a second or two to deploy them.

4. Defend yourself immediately if a bear is in your personal space for any reason. Skip the meet and greet and go straight to a horn blast with bear spray aimed and ready. Then you can do a dominant retreat. (bear dance.)

5. All other situations with a buffer of distance between you and the bear should be handled as follows:

a. Do a meet and greet shout out with a slow wave of an arm. Keep your voice deep, low and loud.

b. Several loud hand claps. Make sure you have his full attention.

c. Stomp the ground hard, slap your thigh loudly. Do this several times if the situation allows.

d. Get your horn clenched firmly in your teeth, bear spray out, ready and aimed.

e. Keep your eyes on the bear while backing away. Keep slapping your thigh and stomping one foot while   retreating slowly. Stomp slap! Stomp slap! Now you're dancing away.

f. Back up until the bear leaves, or you are out of sight. Always retreat in the direction you came   from   to avoid getting any closer to something the bear might be defending.

g. Anytime you have had an uncomfortable encounter with a bear, you need to leave the area and   stay away. Bears often return, don't be there.

THE NEVER EVER LIST

The following are things you should *NEVER* do. Always avoid any behavior that could trigger a predator/prey response.

a. Never scream, whimper, moan or make any high pitched sounds. No blubbering.

b. Don't run, panic or make senseless, frantic motions. Maintain eye contact with the bear.

c. Try not to pant, hyperventilate, or gasp. Take slow, deep, quiet breaths. Get a grip on your fear.

d. Try not to shit, piss or vomit. If you do, pretend you didn't. It's all about your acting skills.

e. Do not freeze, become unresponsive or play dead. You need to be doing a dominant retreat. Stay in slow motion.

f. Use the bear defensive position only with a mama brownie or grizzly, and only as a last resort if you are actually being mauled and are unable to fight back. All other situations fight like hell. Punch, kick, stomp, gouge the nose or eyes. Use rocks, sticks or anything handy. Target the bears face.

Dogs

Having a dog with you when you encounter a bear complicates the situation. A good dog will get between you and the bear and defend you by barking, growling and holding his ground. I would not recommend setting your dog on the bear unless your dog is well trained. A dog that panics and comes running back to his master is apt to have a pissed off bear in hot pursuit. Do *not* sleep with a dog in your tent. A dog belongs outside of the tent on guard duty. A dog in the tent with you is nothing more than a potential food item for the bear. Don't sleep with food!

Using Lethal Force

If you are certain you are having a predatory encounter, shoot a bear only when other options have been exhausted. First use the horn and bear spray if you are able to. Fire at least one warning shot if the situation allows it. Predatory behavior can sometimes be switched off when met with a proactive and vigorous defense. But not always.

A bear sniffing around your tent at night will usually be there only briefly, then move on. If a bear is lingering in your campsite, you should use your horn and/or bear spray first. If a bear won't leave or comes back, you have a possible predatory situation and should consider shooting the bear. If you are in a small backpacking tent, exit and move to open ground so you can see them coming and have the opportunity to defend yourself.

If he starts to claw into your tent, shoot him right through the tent. Exit the tent and finish the job. Once you have decided to kill a bear you need to make sure you do. Wounded bears are extremely dangerous.

Bear Dance Review

1. Meet and greet all bears that are a comfortable distance from you with ;

a. Loud, deep shout

b. A slow wave of your arm overhead

c. Clap your hands a couple times

2. If a bear is 25 ft. or less from you or is charging you;

a. Skip the meet and greet

b. Blow your horn immediately, long and loud!

c. At the same time be aiming your bear spray as a back-up if necessary. Use it if you feel it is appropriate. (short bursts)

d. Now you can start a dominant retreat. Keep blowing the horn until they leave or you are safe.

3. Dance away. Slap your thigh hard, stomp your foot loudly, take a step back. Always face the bear as you retreat. Repeat these steps until you are safely away.

4. Always leave the scene of a confrontation. Depart the way you came if possible to avoid possibly encroaching on something the bear might be defending, seen or not.

Thanks!

Thank you for reading this book. It is both a companion volume and a condensation of my other book on bear safety: "A Handful of Idiots and a Bunch of Bears." The idea was to create a smaller guide on just the essential information you need to know. Please see my other book if you enjoy lots of humorous and true stories to illustrate the points being made about bear safety.

Your Opinions Count

If you enjoyed this book, or even if you didn't, please write an online review for it on Amazon, it would be very much appreciated. Independent writers depend on your input and feedback to improve and promote their work. Be a collaborator and make your opinions known!

Contact Me

I am available for presentations and workshops on "Bear Safety," and "Living in Harmony with Bears." I am also willing to listen to your stories, discuss theory or answer your questions. There is a yahoo group that has been created for this purpose. I am looking forward to hearing from you.

http://groups.yahoo.com/group/adventures-with-bears

Disclaimer

This booklet represents the experiences and opinions of the author. I cannot take any responsibility for your future interactions with bears. The art and science of bear behavior is an ever-expanding body of knowledge. Consequently, the information in this book can never be the final word in this constantly evolving endeavor.